The gods have spoken

By

Vincent Uduh

Mircent Concept

To order copies please contact the publisher.

Email: mircentconcept@ymail.com

ISBN: 978-978-923-499-8

This book is a work of fiction.
Places, events, and situations
in this story are purely fictional.
Any resemblance to actual persons,
living or dead, is coincidental

DEDICATION

I dedicate this book to the suffering children of the world and particularly to that poor African child

CHARACTERS

Irobosa   - The Oba
Omoefe-   Ejiro's mother
Usoro-   Eloho's mother   ——   Irobosa's wives
Obenefe- Oviemuno's mother

Ejiro
Eloho   Irobosa's sons
Oviemuno

Efosa   -   Chief Elder
Osamudiam
Omogeva
Agiri   ——   Obene Elders
Nogeu
Osaede

Ababi Elders
Itonhosa
Onorinode
Agagu
Niji   ——   Abaii Elders

Nwaye
Aubethe

Oghale   -   famous drunkard

Attendants on the Oba.

Villagers

Priests

Warriors

PRODUCTION NOTE

The gods have spoken, is a tragedy which conceived from hatred and wickedness that later beget calamity on Ababi.

Ababi was a big town made up of two villages, Abaii and Obene, named after the son and daughter respectively of a great warrior - Ababi.

The people of Ababi are warriors and great farmers. They are well watered by heavy downpour of rain. During the dry seasons, they relied on the never-disappointing Obene river believed to be Obene- one of their ancestors. Ababi, Abaii and Obene, were generally worshiped and were offered sacrifices as the gods of the land.

Ababi is a prominent town amongst its neighbours and had a large market square at its centre where surrounding villages assemble every fortnight to buy and sell food stuffs mainly oil palm and tuber food crops, largely produced by the great farmers of Ababi.

At the Oba's place were displayed, some marvelous statues of the Obas and great men that ever lived in Ababi. Entering the palace, one would see the beautifully carved royal seat for the Oba directly opposite the front entrance. To its right and left are arrayed side-by-side, six carved chairs for the twelve elders of Ababi: six from Obene and six from Abaii. Outside, for behind the Oba's palace is a native African shrine, which nobody else goes into except the Priest-who consults the gods of the land. Inside the shrine, were the bronze status of Ababi (god of thunder) at the middle, Abaii (god of rain) to its right, and Obene (god of river) to its left —all placed beside the wall. Furthermore, behind the shrine is the beginning of a thick forest called "the forbidding forest" where anyone condemned by the gods would be hanged.

Ababi is ruled by a monarch. From a royal family Abaii emerges the Oba and after the Oba's death, his first son takes over the throne. In Obene, the Chief Elder has his own palace where he meets with the elders before meeting with the Oba when necessary. It has almost the same look as the Oba's palace except for the absence of the Oba's royal seat.

DRESS CODE FOR THE CAST

The **Oba** should tie around his waist a big wrapper which should fold at little above the waist, leaving the chest bare. He wears big neck beads of traditional chiefs and six native wrist beads each on both hands. He must always go on bare feet.

The **Elders** should have wrappers around their waists as desired and big native beads on their necks leaving their chests bare and are bare-footed.

The **Oba's wives** should have around them, the familiar native broad cloth which is wrapped and folded just above the breasts leaving the shoulders bare. They wear native neck beads and the feet are bare.

Oghale, the drunkard, should also reflect his drunkenness in his ways of talking and movement. He should dress like a native palm wine tapper always looking alcoholic.

The **Attendants** in the Oba's palace should dress casually like native young men.

The **Priest** should be costumed with white chalk on his face to look just like a native doctor carrying out a ritual.

Slow mournful music should be played at the events of death to create a sad atmosphere and may be done with drumbeating. Other music should be preferably played on flute and on percussion or string instruments when necessary except for joyful moments when any music to thrill the atmosphere is preferably required.

STRATEGIC FLASHBACK

The traditional solemnity of the Oba(s) of Ababi. "An Oba should have a son to succeed him," was what led to Oba Irobosa's wicked actions. After having his first and second wives-Omoefe and Usoro respectively, who could only give him female children, he went for the wife of a prominent hunter in Obene, who he later killed.

Obenefe, Oba Irobosa's third wife bore him a son Oviemuno. After a year, Omoefe conceived and bore a boy who she named Ejiro. The following year, Usoro gave birth to Eloho a boy. Then there lived a wrathful cold war on whose son will fall into the Oba's shoes. Mainly between the first and the third wives.

Unfortunately Ejiro could't see beyond fifteen years of his life and Omoefe, claimed that Obenefe killed her son. The war turned hot that it nearly became the village idle talk. So the Oba sent Oviemuno on exile to the neighbouring village in order to create peace in the royal family.

It then happened, on a very dark and cold night that the Oba and his attendants walked to the front of the palace on the Oba's quest to catch a view of the dark; a sudden strong wind blew followed by a powerful lightning which lit the entire village for a second. There and then came a great devastating thunder storm which shook the entire village from its very foundation and left just the Oba and his two attendants dead.

Meanwhile, at the Chief elder's palace, Efosa and Oghale were chatting. The cup of palmwine in Oghale's hand fell due to the tremor and they were terrified. There and then, the drunkard told Efosa that those events were not unconnected to Oba Irobosa's wicked attitudes towards the villages and his disobedience to the gods. But Efosa refused to agree and alleged the drunkard's words to one of his frivolous sayings.

After the Oba's burial (with three human heads one for each god), Ejiro's mother connived with Eloho's mother to put Eloho as the next Oba. They met with some Abaii elders who they promised some mouth watering gift if they worked to make Eloho the Oba. These elders in turn ordered the Priest to dance to their tune.

ACT ONE

SCENE 1

(It is now a forthnight after Oba Irobosa's funeral ceremonies. At the Oba's palace, Efosa calls the elders' meeting. The men are sitting as usual. The atmosphere is tense when Efosa gets up to speak).

EFOSA: (clears his throat) Mighty elders of Obene, great elders of Abaii, men of Ababi, I welcome you.

(The elders respond by nodding their heads and with slight talks). We all know that Oba Irobosa had joined his great ancestors and we have played our part by giving him an honourable burial as a great Oba. For as our fathers say; it is not good to talk bad about the dead, so may his soul rest in peace. *(bows his head and the elders do the same).* Now that he had gone, we need to have someone to replace him and this must be one of his sons. Yes, for even in the kingdom of the termites, they have a king. So in my opinion, we should go and bring home his first son, Oviemuno, to take over his father's throne or what do you think? Since I can't tell the minds of the god?

(Pause and sits down).

NIJI: (*stands*) Great elders of Ababi, I great you all. Our people say, "It is the son who follows his father to the farm that could inherit the farm when his father dies".

Oviemuno, indeed is the first son of the late Oba, but he had not been with his father for long before he was taken to the neighbouring village and thus does not even know to the best of my knowledge the rules of this land. And I am very sure that the gods would not accept him that does not know them to govern then (*pauses and sits*).

ITONHOSA: Men of Ababi I greet you all (*stands*). I see things from Niji's perspective. Oviemuno won't and should not be allowed to rule Ababi for one second, because his father sent him out of this village. It was the same Oba Irobosa, who said that "it is he who worked with him that would eat with him." And these words of his must had been meant to solve the problem of who should take over from him. Eloho had been with his father until his last day, when he joined his ancestors and so should be crowned the Oba of Ababi (pauses and sits and *side talks resume*).

AGIRI: (*rising slowly with some angry looks*). People of Ababi, let's not deceive ourselves. Our fathers say that "An elderly person cannot be at home and watch the goats starve to death". An abomination is about to happen in the land of Ababi. It has never been done and would never happen successfully without facing the wrath of the gods. If it is that Oviemuno is dead, it would have been a different case, but he lives and you want to topple him and bring down the anger of the gods on our land. No! I won't be part of it o!

NIJI: (*stands*) If so, let us call in the Priest to go and consult the gods on this issue for the best solution to this misunderstanding and (*Priest enters, through the front door*). …We want you to consult the gods on who should take over the throne of the Oba, either Oviemuno or Eloho (*pauses and sits*).

(*The priest leaves through the front door*).

AGIRI: Please note that the reason why Oviemuno was taken to the neighbouring village was to create in the royal family a peaceful atmosphere, since the Oba's wives were at loggerheads, especially between the first wife Omoefe and the third Obenefe. Omoefe believed that Obenefe killed her late son, Ejiro. So I strongly believe that the Oba's words that it is he who worked with him that would eat with him, has nothing to do with who would ascend the throne after him.

Hmm, may it not be that Omoefe and Usoro have hands in what is happening here today. (*Pauses and sits*).

EFOSA: (*to the attendant*) Okay, call in the three wives of late Oba Irobosa so that they may testify for themselves.

(*The attendant goes outside, the three wives of the late Oba come in shoulder to shoulder, they pay courtesy quickly and remained on their knees*).

You were all called in here to answer just what you were asked when it is time for you to talk. Okay! Now, to you Omoefe, why were you at loggerheads with Obenefe?

OMOEFE: It was because her jealousy made her kill my dear son, Ejiro and…

OBENEFE: (*interrupts*) it is a lie! Ejiro died the death of his god, and never did I even have such evil intention of…

EFOSA: (*angry*) Enough! Didn't I say you answer only when you were asked to? Okay, Obenefe, now your turn, what did you think made the Oba send Oviemuno and not Eloho to the neighbouring village?

OBENEFE: That was because Oviemuno was older and more matured than Eloho and could read the real situation of things (*pauses*).

USORO: It is a lie, the presence of Oviemuno would have inspired Obenefe to kill Eloho too!

EFOSA: Okay! Enough! It seems you don't want to abide by my rules. So we've heard enough from you all, you can now take your leave.

(*The three women take their leave. The Priest enters through the front door with his back, as a man blowing a flute comes after him into the palace. He turns his face to the elders and speaks*).

PRIEST: The gods said that Oviemuno would not sit on their throne because he had not been with them and would not be able to serve them with all his heart. Thus, it should fall on the head of Eloho as the next Oba, due to Ejiro's death. (*Turns and leaves*)

ITONHOSA: (*stands and laughs*) I said it! The gods are not dead and they are not blind. (*Sits and smiles*).

EFOSA: Great men of Ababi, you have all seen and heard from the horse's mouth. Eloho in a fortnight would be coronated as the Oba. But I must say here that the repercussion or price if you like, for any wrong act could only be deferred but must be paid. Yes, for an elder won't, because a child wants eat an egg, involves himself in stealing…

AGAGU: (*interrupts*) Efosa! Efosa!! I would like you to be understood, because you speak too much in proverbs…ehh!

OSAEDE: I would like to stand in here for Efosa, we are not so sure of what is happening here, we know the Priest has said what he heard from the gods but proverb, we say, is a lamp for searching the dark.

EFOSA: Yes Osaede, if not for the foolish, all discussions would be done in proverbs. For our fathers say that "Nobody can attempt to pick his eyes with the same object he uses to pick his teeth", yes, if he does, he knows the possible results. We don't want to be dragged into a fire for any reason. A farmer who brings into his house ant-infested firewood, does not only invite the ants into his house but also the lizard. Repercussion once again may not come when one expects it to. So let us abide by the words of the gods, since real people as we are now, don't gather together to talk foolishly but act wisely. (*pause*).

(*The elders leave the place in their ones and twos*).

SCENE 2

(The fortnight is here, at the Oba's palace are gathering: the elders all sitting as usual, the wives of the late Oba were sitting behind the Abaii elders. The people of Ababi are present-some inside and the others outside the palace. Eloho stands beside the Oba's royal seat. Every one present leaves space where the drummers and a group of dancers will perform.   In their brief appearance before the commencement of the ceremony, it should be apparent that they comprise some female dancers to compliment the male.   Few minutes later, the dancers should dance off and the music should continue quite audibly and shortly afterwards they should fade away as Efosa begins to talk)

EFOSA: (*stands*) People of Ababi, I greet you all, great elders of Ababi, I greet you all, my fellow villagers I welcome you to this memorable ceremony of our time…

(*The villagers respond with shouts*)… we all know the laws of the land, that after one Oba comes another. Oba Irobosa had joined his great ancestor; he too has become one of our ancestors. Now, one of his sons is going to replace him as the Oba. The elders of this land have joined heads together and acceded to agree that Eloho, instead of Oviemuno would be coronated on the Oba's Royal seat today before you all. Here, he is standing besides his late father's royal seat and also before us, ready to serve this land and the gods. I am going to ask him some questions before you all and to your hearing will he answer them. For our fathers say that "It is better done openly so that it would be clear to both the hen and the goat".

(*Eloho comes and stands in between the two rows of elders and bows his head*).

Yes, people of Ababi, I would now talk on your behalf and as an elders of this great land. Eloho, are you ready to carry the task of ruling Ababi as an Oba?

ELOHO: Yes I am.

EFOSA: Can we trust you to defend our course and maintain the glory of Ababi?

ELOHO: Yes, you can.

EFOSA: How about our gods, will you continue to maintain the cordial relationship between our gods and us?

ELOHO: Yes, I will.

EFOSA: Dear people of Ababi, I believe you all heard right?

VILLAGERS: Yes! Yes!! (*Suddenly, Oghale forces his way into the presence of the elders*).

OGHALE: No! No!! It is a big lie! We're doomed! We're
doomed!!

Don't let it happen, the wrath of the gods is already on us
except Oviemuno the first son of Irobosa is crowned the Oba.
(*Two men pull him out even as he continues to talk*).

NIJI: Take him out! Take him out of here, he is a drunkard and
has nothing to offer.

ITONHOSA: (*Laughs*) He thinks we are discussing about how to
drink here, shameless old thing.
(*Efosa remains speechless as he watches Oghale being
dragged out of the palace*).

EFOSA: Okay! Dear people of Ababi, let us continue to carry out
the enthronement of our new Oba…
(*Eloho knees down as Efosa goes nearer to him holding the
Oba's crown over him*).
Our people say that the head which is destined to wear a
king's crown will surely be crowned one day. So may the
head below the crown be that which the gods want. May the
gods of our land be with Eloho, may they be behind him and
not opposing him. May he trample on his enemies and may
his foes remain under his feet.

May his regime be glorious and splendid and may the splendor be seen all over the face of the earth. May the gods of our ancestors lead him (*Pause and puts the crown on Eloho's head*).

(All the villagers all bow and say, "Ise." Efosa then went outside with Obenefe to meet Oghale who is standing alone).

OGHALE: We are finished! I see this great land fall and to the worst of it all, you Efosa of all people disappointed me! You surprised me. In short you proved me wrong to have thought of you to be different from those nuisances who call themselves wise men and sit in the front of the assembly representing their heads-which have run out of ideas. But you proved your indifference and now it is as vivid as the rising sun that we have nobody to stand for us when we would need wise men. For no reason should Eloho be coronated the Oba while Oviemuno is still alive and healthy. Oh! A taboo, an abomination has taken root and evil has eaten deep into our kingdom (sober).

EFOSA: Enough of your wise talks, I know you can see but I won't be an exception to oppose the gods of our ancestors and face the repercussion. I still have seen some doubts and also have my plans…

OBENEFE: What are these your plan?

EFOSA: Just relax and hear me out. I know it is dangerous for a man to let his cat out of the bag at times like this, because everywhere is crowded and catching it back won't be so easy if at all Oviemuno would be brought back to this village, this will surely go a long way to create an atmosphere of doubts in the people's mind. Then they would see for themselves that Oviemuno really is alive.

Oghale: Hmm! Are you sure this is not a practical joke?

Efosa: No, you just trust me and give me your full support when necessary.
(Efosa and Obenefe return to the palace while Oghale remains outside. Inside the palace, music goes on audibly and both the dancers and the drummers are at their peak of excitement, drumming and dancing with all their strength. Later the sounds fade and the shouts wear gradually to its minimum).

SCENE 3

(Next two market days, the Oba calls the elders to convene. Beside the wall near the front entrance sitting on the floor helplessly, is the Priest who now has a sudden attack of leprosy and big boils all over his body. Music starts playing audibly as the Oba enters through the door behind close to his royal seat. At this, the elders stand. The Oba walks, turns back and walks towards his royal seat. On getting there, he turns to face the elders and sits down. After this, the elders also sit. Music fades away as the Oba begins to talk).

ELOHO: *(sits)* Great men of Abaii, mighty men of Obene, I greet you all. Great elders of Ababi I welcome you. Indeed, I called for this meeting; I know you may wonder why, since the call was a little sudden. My father said, "he won't wait for the rain before watering his dying seedlings". Why I said this is because of the sudden call. I regret every inconvenience it might have caused you. If you look behind you, at the other end of the palace you will find a man cursed by the gods, a man who would not be left among the living, a man whose deeds were considered evil by the gods and so the gods had poured out wicked diseases on him-leprosy and boils...

(The elders look at the Priest, shaking their heads).

...Yes! He must have offended the gods. *(Pauses).*

AGIRI: (*stands*) May your highness live forever. I want to say something and want you all to hear me out this man is the one who consults the gods of our land, what on earth had he done that could bring on him this evil, dreaded disease? What on earth could he have done to bring on him the wrath of our gods, that couldn't have been misinterpreting or possibly saying what the gods did not tell him. This could be very dangerous not just to him alone but to any of us involved, because our father's say, "The rising sun, though will first fall on the person standing in front, it will later set on the one sitting behind him".

NIJI: (*With anxious look, he stands*) No! No!! So much in proverbs, Agiri must be pointing at someone here indirectly. I want him to do come out openly and clear the bushes before us. Let him be blunt and stop beating about the bush for we are no puppies (*sits*).

EFOSA: (*stands*) May your highness see ripe old age, I would like to stand in here for Agiri because I am in support of what he just said, If Niji knows that he is the person sitting behind this helpless man, then he should happily let us know. But if otherwise, then why let himself be disturbed by what Agiri said? He should be silent and watch who the sun, as Agiri said, will set on. Now, your highness, what are we to do with this man?

ELOHO: Yes, he shouldn't be among the living any longer. He will be taken to the forbidding forest where he will remain until his death and his assistant will take his position as directed by the gods. Then the assistant being the Priest should consult the gods and tell us what they said concerning the cursed man.

(Two attendants come out at this command and carried the leprosy stricken man out of the palace as music indicating sadness begins to play audibly. A minute later, Oviemuno enters the palace standing before all present as they mope at him with great surprise. Music fades out gradually as Efosa breaks the silence).

OVIEMUNO: Great elders of Ababi, I greet you all. I know I came at the right time because I was believed to be dead or ignorant of the great land and the people of Ababi. Yes! Many now think I no longer exist while others think I was sent to the neighbouring village because of my non-desire to take over my late father's throne. I know you all here knew why I was sent out. Or if you were ignorant of it, relax and hear me out, my father said this to me, "You are my eldest son and you I cherish the most. Though I have my other son but because of your age and knowledge you are going to leave for the neighbouring village for I want no harm on you since you will rule after me." After my father's death, I was informed to come and be coronated as his successor. I arrived only to hear that my younger brother has assumed the throne. For this reason, have I come so that you who heard false information about me would be cleared, likewise the villagers too... (*The new Priest enters costumed just like the former. Before him his assistant blowing a flute, this makes Oviemuno to pause*).

PRIEST: Good news have reached the land and our land would be at peace again says the gods; if only what they wanted and directed were done, The gods told me to tell you all these, "I am the god of this land, I fought for you when you were asleep and I provided for you when others were starving. Oviemuno! Oviemuno!! Oviemuno!!! should and must be crowned as the Oba to succeed Irobosa who had joined us, so that peace and harmony would reappear in Ababi. If not so done, Abaii the god of rain would seize the rain, Obene the god of river would dry up and then your harvest will be hopeless and your land would face serious drought- if you refuse to abide by the words of the ancient-warrior, Ababi the god of thunder." Those were the words of the gods to you, the choice remains yours. (*Pause and back the Oba about to leave the palace*).
(*Everybody present is amaze and looks at one another mysteriously*).

ELOHO: (gathers himself up) Come back here! You think you can just say any thing anyhow and get away with it? You have come to cause confusion and great uncertainty here! It has never happened before. I have never heard or witnessed such so I won't accept it. The gods cannot call the same cock white today and black tomorrow. No! They are gods? They are as constant as the northern star in all they say and do. So you wicked Priest, you must have misinterpreted the gods or even say what you did not hear and this is equal to death sentence by hanging on the trees of the forbidden forest. This would be executed with immediate effect before the wrath of the gods rain like fire burning with sulphur on us.

EFOSA: (*stands slowly*) Your highness, why pass death sentence on him so quickly, how about if he was right and you are wrong after all?

ITONHOSA: It does not baffle me any longer, I know you are always made to oppose the right thing Efosa and you would support him. So I'm not surprised at it okay!

NIJI: The Oba was quite correct, this priest would have said what he said because of some gift which must have been rashly promised when we said, we don't want he that does not know our gods and the penalty of causing someone to offend the gods to be our Oba. So he should be hung right away as directed by the Oba.

AGIRI: My hands are not in this man's death... O!

ELOHO: (*with morbid look on his face*) He should be hanged right away and his assistant should take over his position. (*Pause and stands, walks out of the palace through the door behind while the elders are all standing. The condemned man is taken out of the palace as the elders leave the palace through the front door. Sonorous music plays audibly indicating a sad atmosphere.*)

ACT TWO
SCENE 1

(At the Oba's palace. In the next fortnight in the evening, the Oba and the elders are sitting. The atmosphere is tense).

ELOHO: Dear people of Ababi, I greet you all and welcome you all. Our fathers said that who ever desires the king's honour must not go against the laws of the land. The laws of our land had been trampled on and we know that in this land we have the gods and these gods must not be offended at all.

The gods of the land have said and must be obeyed that Oviemuno had called down their wrath on his head for corrupting to death their Priest and thus must face death…

(The elders show surprise and side talks begin).

Yes, that's it, that's just what the gods want and even I can't stop it. I would have if I could for he is my brother.

EFOSA: Great men of Ababi, I am sorry to say this, it seems each time we are called here, it is just to tell us that one person or the other had been condemned by the gods for one reason or the other. We say, one can't predict the temper of the chick inside the egg until it is hatched. Ever since Oba Eloho was crowned, we have not talked much about the development of our land and the betterment of our villagers. Things are going wrong at the highest speed and we seemed to have turned the blind eye to them. Is this what the reign of Oba Eloho has in its purse for Ababi? If so, then our teeth have touched a stone and each of us who hasn't felt it would certainly feel it where no dialogical solution would be applicable. I am so sorry to have said this but it is the truth. I don't think I will be a party to these unilateral policies of Oba Eloho. I would like to take an excuse first to ease myself.

(Efosa leaves the palace through the front door and finds Oviemuno coming into the palace; he stops him).

EFOSA: Oviemuno! Oviemuno!! Oviemuno!!! How many times did I call you?

OVIEMUNO: Three times.

EFOSA: Oviemuno, may I be the last person to see you in this land from today, leave the village and don't return until I send for you or you will see yourself facing death. Eloho has condemned you to death claiming the gods wants you dead, though I can't say but leave.

OVIEMUNO: (stares at Efosa in utter suprise) Really?

EFOSA: Leave! And don't come back for anything for your own good. But bear it in mind that he whose head is destined to wear a king's crown will surely be crowned one day. Leave!

(Oviemuno leaves and Efosa returns to the palace).

NWAYE: Efosa, thank the gods that you are back. I have to tell you something as an old man, though you are also one. We say that a child ignorant of the deadly power of a juju calls it a vegetable. Not that I calling you a baby but you behaved like one, for allowing your tongue to voice out what you said before going to ease yourself. The gods are not crazy and he who thought of the gods to be crazy is surely out of his mind.

EFOSA: Nwaye, mark you, I will stand by my words and will stick to them till I join my ancestors.

AGIRI: It is important and also necessary for me to say here, that I am on Efosa's side and behind him will I remain because such daily condemnation is becoming a habit and never happened so frequently in the days of our past Obas.

ELOHO: I heard all you've said but will still say that I would have stopped Oviemuno's condemnation if I could. But I don't want to bring the wrath of the gods on us and thus will obey their request as had been directed.

After this meeting, Oviemuno would be brought forward and offered to the gods for peace and unity among the people of Ababi. We would mourn him for good forth can days, despite the fact that such dead should note be mourned.

AGIRI: But I thought you said you didn't want the wrath of the gods on us, then why do you want to do what is not done by mourning a forbidden dead?

ELOHO: Okay, as you want, he won't be mourned (*stands and leave the palace through the door behind while the elders are standing and mournful music plays audibly*).

SCENE 2

(After the harvest period, all the elders of Ababi are complete and sitting as usual in the Oba's palace. The music plays as the Oba comes into the palace through the door behind. The elders stand up, the Oba walks to the centre of the wide space between the two roles of the elders before returning to his royal seat. The elders sit).

ELOHO: (*clears his throat*) Great men of Ababi I great you all, I welcome you to this palace where solutions to problems confronting the land and people of Ababi are found. I'm speaking first because I have to as the Oba of Ababi, but I was not the one who called for the meeting but Efosa. He may now tell us the reason.

EFOSA: (*stands*) Great men of Ababi I greet you all. I welcome you most sincerely because I have some words for us. The sea owns the tides and the land praises it for that, but when the sea fails to check its tides and it over flows onto the land, then the land abuses the sea. We people of Ababi are farmers and our prominence cannot be taken for a cock and bull tale. From the east to the west as the sun rise and sets, and from the south to the north as the trade winds blow so are we remembered daily in the minds of all who are close to us and even those afar. They see and hear about us directly or otherwise, but we are now tirelessly working this unconditional situation into a predicament. They say that the easiest way to get rid of someone is to call him big names and if he allows worm and insects to feed on his taproot, then he will fall. As I said, our prominence is as vivid as the bright daylight and we are called mighty names because of it, but it seems we have carried the pride on our shoulders forgetting that the next step awaiting us is how and where to fall on…

ITONHOSA: (*interrupts*) Efosa, if you don't have something reasonable to say, tell us and stop beating about the bush. We have better things to do.

AGIRI: (*stands*) Itonhosa, for no reason whatsoever should you have challenged Efosa, he has been saying the right things and understood him. Proverb, indeed they say is the salt for a good talk and when not used, the words become tasteless. So, if you feel you are not one of us here, then you go! Or better still, turn your deaf ear to his words. (*sits*)

ITONHOSA: Okay, I can see you are the fly following after Efosa's anus. I suggest you watch yourself or in his mess you will die!

ELOHO: No! Men of Ababi, I will not allow such insult to continue. We have had enough. Efosa should be allowed to plant his seeds as he wishes, as long as he plants rightly.

EFOSA: Great men of Ababi, I cannot plant well without using my hoe and cutlass because with them I can do excellent planting. As I was saying, the harvest have come and gone. Long before now, in times like this, our village will be filled with harvested tubers and palm fruit and people from other village visits us like ants visit the sugar. But our land has refused to yield. Our great river has sized flowing! Rain refused to fall on our soil! Hmm, what have we done wrong that our people should starve?

NIJI: Abomination!

EFOSA: What a shame on us to starve! I mean going to beg or even buying what we used to produce in abundance…

ELOHO: Never!

EFOSA: What then, a taboo? What a shame on the land flowing with milk and honey turning into a desert. Yes because as the yam peels the knife knows.
Anybody here who says he is blind or deaf to all these and that the gods are not seriously angry with us deceives his own mind. (*Pauses and sits*).

ELOHO: Yes, as a matter of fact, Efosa is very right and has said all we need to know. The gods are angry and something urgently needs to be done to correct the decadence of our tradition before it deteriorates to what we would not be able to control. Indeed an abomination was committed and its repercussion is now facing us…

(E*lders react silently looking at one another*).

…Yes, the gods requested for Oviemuno, they wanted him sacrificed to them because of what he did, which you all know and could testify to…

(*Oghale enters the palace looking drunk as usual*).

NIJI: Wha…what have you come here to do? Were you invited or you think here is under the pyramid where you get drunk? (*Elders stare at Oghale*).

OGHALE: That is enough! Do you think you are better than me? Who on earth told you that? Or is because you sit here each time among the elders and watch their lips dance that made you think you are better? I am here to speak for the villagers, our people who you pretend to be standing for. They are now starving because of what you did to have crowned the wrong person as be the Oba, when Oviemuno is still very much alive.

AUBETHE: Take him out! Take him out! He's drunk and knows not his left from his right. I pity you because you don't know what you're doing.

(Two attendants come to drag Oghale out of the palace).

OGHALE: Taking me outside does not end it and would not. It will only worsen everything and even you Aubethe, won't be saved because I see you senseless monster in trouble if you don't take your time.

ELOHO: Leave him alone! Leave him. The gods brought him here not for what he just finish saying but so that he could hear for himself if he really has ears. We say it is good to show the dog its faults for beating it just in case of next time. I was saying some things about the abomination committed, why we suffered poor harvest and drought and I said Oviemuno should be offered as a sacrifice to the gods.

OGHALE: (*interrupts*) Abomination! Can never happen!

ELOHO: I know you will say so. Efosa and you Oghale led Oviemuno away after you learnt of what the gods said. Out of ignorance you denied the gods of what was theirs, especially, Oghale who deceived the men I sent to get hold of Oviemuno. You were fighting for selfish interest and honour where you did not sow one. Indeed, I pity you because you know not the weight of what you did but Efosa indeed cannot deny his knowledge about the consequences surrounding such act.

EFOSA: I beg your pardon, your highness. I for one told Oviemuno to leave the village for his life was surrounded by wild and heart less animals-since I don't and still won't support your act of dictatorship. Oghale, to the best of my knowledge, knew nothing about the escape of Oviemumo and so you have failed for wanting to lay blame on an innocent head.

OGHALE: That is how he does, he shouldn't have been the Oba, and that is why he wants Oviemuno dead, isn't it? Answer me!

ITONHOSA: I hope that is enough of your drunken rage and utterances…
(*The Priest enters with a man blowing a flute*).

PRIEST: The gods want everybody to learn where he went wrong. The hawk does not swoop down on the chick for sport and the gods won't pardon anybody who fights for selfish aims. They say a river does not flow backwards-abomination! A leg that walks zig-zag has a zig-zag eye watching it. Yes for it is easy to assume madness, but how about the trekking involved." I would summarily explain all these to you. Do not be too carefree and put your hand on what you cannot carry or should you, think of yourself too wise for any one to get rid of. The gods have called for the replacement of Oviemuno before things can get back on the right track. Oghale has been picked by the gods to replace Oviemuno since he involved himself in Oviemuno escape.

(*Silent reactions from the elders*).

EFOSA: This is absurd (stands). No! It can't go down well with me. It can never be done, never! Never!! It is as if anybody who apposes Oba Eloho should get prepared for his funeral. He knows how he colluded with the so-called Priest-who knew nothing, consulted nothing but forged lies! I won't give into it this time around even if I am left alone or things would go from bad to worse.

OGHALE: Does he think I would beg for mercy? No! Never!! For what? I am in the land of my ancestors, where I will live and when dead, I died to join them. You think I fear death? No, someone at fifty-five has tried in life. After all, some young kids die in their twenties for nothing. But I will die for the sake of my fatherland, for the sake of my people and for the sake of the gods' will. Tell me, is it not a hero's death? Go ahead and kill me, so that I won't talk against your bad attitudes. You heartless thing! But I will fight for my people from the world of the dead. (*He moves to take his leave*).

ELOHO: Get hold of him before he disappears and another abomination would happen. Get hold of him! At least the Priest is here and you heard it from him, Get hold of him and bind him up until the next market day when he would be offered to the gods for peace and progress in our land.
(*Two attendants hold Oghale who struggles with them. They tie Oghale up and carry him out of the palace through the front door. Total silence covers the palace*).

NOGEU: What did I hear you say, your highness? (*Rises on his feet*) Did you say for peace and progress or do you really mean for war and disaster? Efosa had said that he was totally responsible for Oviemuno's escape since he did not believe you. But the gods through the Priest said Oghale was responsible, are the gods dead can't they see, hear and speak correctly anymore? Or do you want tell me that Efosa knowing the full penalty of what he said must have lied? Who between Efosa and the gods is lying?

ONORINODE: (stands) doesn't that mean you doubt the gods? Does it? So if you were left alone Nogeu, you won't know who is lying? Then why are you here, if the laws of our land are not written in your mind as an elder. Everybody here knows beyond reasonable doubt that Efosa had lied except for those flies that follow after his anus…

AGIRI: (*interrupts*) Enough! Enough of your delusive words. They said he who likes you does not see your faults and that is why you are in support of the Oba's misconduct. Besides, who are those flies after your anus? You'd better select your words right or you'll face the consequence because you know you're the biggest of all fools here!

ELOHO: Enough! Enough of this arrant nonsense! Okay, goodbye and mind your ways (*Rises and takes his leave. All the elders rise, each one showing sign of anger or happiness on their face as they leave the palace. Music plays audibly*).

<h1 style="text-align:center">SCENE 3</h1>

(Two days before the next market day at the Chief of the elders' palace, Efosa calls the five elders of Obene to convene. The men are sitting, the atmosphere is tense).

EFOSA: Great elders of Obene, I welcome you all. I know you may be surprised at this meeting where only six persons are sitting instead of twelve. Just feel at home. I called you here. We were all present at the Oba's palace when Eloho condemned Oghale to death through his so-called Priest-who he pioneers and dictates to on what he should say to get rid of anybody opposing him.

OSAEDE: (*stands*) But I think the Priest says what he hears from the gods and must for no reason be disobeyed?

EFOSA: Yes, Osaede, I love that question especially for now and not at the Oba's palace where they won't allow reasons to prevail because of self-centeredness.
Ever since Eloho was coroneted as the Oba, if not for the fact that I attacked his ill attention to the village welfare matters, we won't have had the opportunity to discuss the present drought engulfing our land. They say I talk too much, but what I say can never be heard from the mouth of any wise man whose knowledge is less than mine. When we were at

the Oba palace, the day Oviemuno entered the palace, didn't the late Priest say that the gods wanted Oviemuno coroneted as his father's successor? You can tell me what happened. The Oba charged him for treason and before you and I he was sent to the great beyond, all because Eloho saw that he said the truth. His predecessor who was used to pronounce Eloho as Oba Irobosa's successor then…

(*silent reactions from the elders*).

…Leprosy! Yes, leprosy and boils enveloped him.

Eloho should not have been enthroned at first!

I knew that the elders of Abaii worked for their selfish interest and you would query me. "Why didn't you disagree and refuse crowning him? But how could I have stood-alone? How could I stand alone when you yourself would have called me a mad and foolish old man and the villagers would have known me for that false belief? I only had to agree because I realized your eyes were covered with a scale and your insight blinded.

NOGEU: (*stands*) Emm, if I may ask I want to know more about Oghale, because I know him to be a drunk, frivolous and one who is merely ridiculous.

EFOSA: Thank you very much Nogeu for that link…I would take it from the scratch because that is the main reason why we are here. Yes, Oghale is an addicted drunk but on the contrary, our people say that "No matter how white a lizard excreta is there is always a blackspot on it." Indeed, Oghale is frivolous and looks ridiculous as you said, but he has an insight and never stops saying what he thinks is right no matter the opposition. People take him to be talking nonsense whenever he speaks and on this ground, the elders of Abaii and their so-called Oba Eloho ride on you all but not me. Seeing that Oghale saw the truth, they planned against him. Take a look at this, never did Niji or Itonhosa, for once, challenged the decisions of Eloho. Rather, they both supported it; because they don't want to block the stream where they drink from. Others may not be so wise to notice what is happening. Eloho chose to kill Oghale, why not me? I thought, I claimed responsibility for Oviemuno's escape? But he knew it wouldn't be so easy for him. That was why he preyed on Oghale, using his poor manners as a smokescreen. So now I want you all to go out and oppose this wicked plans. Where he refuses to compromise with us, something must then be done for revenge. Eloho mustn't continue or we will be slaughtered one after the other

AGIRI: Yes, I have an idea which I think if well executed would bring about a lasting solution to the crisis facing us. Eloho is such a person who likes to prove or rather boast of what he can't do. We say that the python seeking assurance of adulthood measures his length with the palm tree. So we should do what would make Eloho want to prove some stupidity. One can't be bathing inside a river and allow soap to worry his eyes, no!

Eloho had done enough and should not be allowed to go beyond this stage. We should kidnap one of his six elders if he fails to hear our protest…

(*Positive reactions from the elders*).

…Yes, from there he would like to proof a point and we will teach him some lesson. For a tree that does not know how to dance will be taught by the wind.

OMOGEVA: (*stands*). I should come in here. I have heard all you said and would say I'm wholly convinced. But who among the Abaii elders would be used for this savage? (*Pauses and sits*).

AGIRI: (*stands*). Who else among them would be kidnapped to have great impact on Eloho if not Agagu? He is a very close relative to the royal family, I mean to Eloho's mother. Eloho loves Agagu more than any of the Abaii elders and would spend his last strength fighting to get him back. I want to believe that everybody here agrees with what we've said so far…

(*The elders nod*).

…Thus, we thus need a volunteer who will lead some young men to kidnap Agagu as agreed. Who will bell the cat? (Sits).

OSAMUDIAM: Yes (*stands*) emm… I am closer to the youths of Obene and know those among them who are capable of doing such a thing when ordered. So in a nutshell, I volunteer to bell the cat.

EFOSA: Great men of Obene, I am happy and regard your high level of understanding. Let us all keep the egg given to us here in our secret purse for if held carelessly could cost us our lives. Goodbye and stay alert. *(Music plays)*.

SCENE 4

(In the evening of that fateful market day close to the forbidding forest are: the Oba, the elders of Ababi, two attendants and some villagers and Oghale (with both hands tied at his back). Solemn music to indicate mournful atmosphere is audibly playing. A moment later, music fades).

EFOSA: Great men of Ababi, I am still appealing on behalf of Oghale. He had done nothing to deserve death and should be spared, for peace to reign.

NIJI: That is a child's talk Efosa, I thought you have grown out of this childish attitude. Are you appealing for Oghale to us or to the gods? The gods asked for him, here and now he will go to them…

AGIRI: *(interrupts)* Which gods asked for him, ehh? Is it the gods of you and your so-called Oba Eloho? Tell me, I want to know.

ITONHOSA: Niji, Niji! You need not talk to this man; he is just an elder since Obene lacks wise men. The gods have spoken. Let him ask and answer his questions by himself. He portrays the likes of a demented man (turn away from Agiri).

(The ropes are in place and Oghale goes closer to the foot of the tree. Mournful impressions prevail on the faces of the villagers present; some are crying, others cover their faces. Oghale tries to speak).

OGHALE: Let me talk! Let me talk! I think you want to send me out of this world, ehh? Then allow me say my last words on earth. Yes, my fellow villagers, it is a pity that you great farmers are starving. It seems you are sad for me? You should be, but I tell you that this is my happiest day on earth. Not because it is the last but because I have enjoyed all the good things of Ababi, saw great Obas who made life worth living and I won't live to see much disaster come upon Ababi…

(Silent reaction from all present).

Yes! I know he has more words to counter mine and deceive you—this is why he is hanging me today since I said what I saw. I am not appealing for pardon because I have done nothing wrong to deserve death, but as I told you today is my happiest day. Worst days await Ababi in the nearest future. Except Oviemuno is made the Oba, Ababi would turn a deserted land…

(Some elders from Obene nod).

…Goodbye as I join my ancestors, your ancestors. So do not hesitate to fight for your land. I will soon be the past but you are the future.

Remember this day when the famous Oghale was hanged for
you.

*(The attendants tie Oghale's neck with rope-already on the
tree. They pull the rode downwards from one end, the other
end pulls Oghale up. The villagers watch with broken hearts
as tears flow from their eyes. Everybody remaining still,
looking helpless. Music sounds mournfully. A sudden dark
clod covers the sky and strong winds blow from four corners
of the earth, the villagers run home and side talk like "The
gods must be angry because of this!" fade with the villagers
as they disappear. Mighty thunder-storms and great
lightening continue into the night)*

SCENE 5

(The Oba and his two attendants are in the palace. One of the attendants speaks).

ATTENDANT: (*standing on shivering legs*) Hmm! Ob...Oba E... Eloho, your highness, Oghale's death was different o! I have never seen such before. The signs that followed his death were too much and we can still feel some of them now. He...he predicted war and your ousting...

EHOLO: Do you believe him? You better don't. He is a drunk.

ATTENDANT: Your highness, but for days before his death, no wine was given to him. He was not drunk when he made those statements.

ELOHO: (*sudden turns angry*) Look, let me not hear such from you any longer! Oghale was an addicted drunkard and this affected his way of thinking. He made those statements just to deceive the villagers, knowing it was his last day on earth.

ATTENDANT: Your highness, I am sorry to say this. You know that some wounds don't heal and some scares never fade...

ELOHO: (*interrupts*) And then! What is that supposed to mean?

ATTENDANT: Well, the villagers are the people you rule and they
could rebel as I can see…

ELOHO: (interrupts) What can you see?

ATTENDANT: What I heard they villagers murmuring as the left
for home after Oghale's execution. They said, "The gods
must be angry because of this, the gods must be angry,"

(*The Oba and his attendants shake as mighty thunderstorms
rock the land*)

ACT THREE
SCENE 1

(The following day at the Chief of the elders' palace, Efosa calls the Obene elders; the atmosphere is tense).

EFOSA: Great men of Obene, I greet and welcome you. We all saw what happened yesterday and heard what the people said as they ran to their homes. Any action we take now to topple Eloho's regime would go down well with them especially with Obenes. We say that a goat which keeps the company of the dog will soon learn how to eat excrete; and we don't want to learn how to lead people astray or how to call black coloured cloth white. We have been pushed to the wall and you know what is next. We have! Eloho won't be left to pound on our heads. We shouldn't settle for any compromise, should we? We are peace-loving people and now or never, if we really want peace, would better get prepared for war...

(Silent reaction from the elders).

...Yes! I know what I am saying, not that we should go outright to strike first.

But I know and assure you that with Agagu's kidnap, Eloho would declare war against us. That was why I said, if we really want peace in Ababi, then, we should better get really prepared for battle. Our fathers say, "Getting prepared for

something is no sign of fear." So we better prepare because it is going to be tough, but self-confidence and determination will surely see us through to victory. Do not be afraid or discouraged. For, no matter how tough it may be, if the cobwebs unite, they are enough to tie down a lion.
(*The elders nod in agreement*)

AGIRI: (*stands*) Yes, Efosa, you are very correct. I like the way you speak, if we have two of your kind in Ababi, and then things would never go wrong. I share your view and strongly support our getting prepared for a counter offensive. One need not shout on top of his voice before one's words make sense but only that one need talk before people listen to one. Agagu has been kidnapped as you know and the reason for this is to get Eloho on his toes. Yes to get him out of the royal seat! But he can't just leave the throne except he is dead and he can't die without something or some one killing him. Am I making any sense?
(*The elders nod their heads indicating common concent*).
…You see, kidnapping Agagu as we've done would go a long way in bringing this dream to reality (Sits).

NOGEU: (*stands*) Emm, you have talked and we have agreed. We need to get prepared as you said and we need some youth to be trained into warriors to compliment the ones we have. But somebody from here should be with then, so that they will know we are behind them. Who will take that up?

OSAEDE: Yes, you made a good and very important point there. On the issue of who will gear up the youth, I think Osamudiam being very close to the youths will be on the forefront to be assisted by Omogeva. Is this okay?

EFOSA: Well, it can't be okay until the people agree to it.

OSAMUDIAM: Great elders of Obene, what am I an elder for, if I do not put in my strength to serve Obene people? I will say here; as long as it right, I am ready to play my part excellently.

OMOGEVA: Great elders of Obene, I greet you all. On my own part, I have nothing much to add than agreeing with the proposal. I will assist Osamudiam with all I have.

EFOSA: Yes! I love the way you showed your high level of understanding. Let it be as we have agreed (*he pauses*). On the other hand, as we want Oviemuno as the Oba, then Eloho must die. Obenefe is now in danger and should be brought back home safely.

OSAEDE: Yes, I am very close to her and would take up the task of bringing her safe back home safe and sound.

EFOSA: I thank you all, great men of Obene, your support and encouragement will surely sail Obene out of this trouble water. You shall never be forgotten for your high level of understanding and selfless service for the survival of Obene and Ababi as a whole. May the gods of our land be with you and me, so that we can achieve our set goals.

THE ELDERS: Amen!

(*The elders rise to leave while music plays audibly*).

SCENE 2

(Two days later, at the Oba's palace, the Oba calls the elders of Abaii. The men are all sitting in a row except Agagu. The atmosphere is very tense).

ELOHO: Great elders of Abaii, I welcome you all. Emm, I called you and would say if asked, that you should know why you are here. The mother hen whose chick was taken won't hesitate to go for it, even if it has ten of them. We all know that the Abaii elders are not complete. Among you is missing one of our great men- Agagu- who I really don't know where he is but know he wouldn't have embarked on any journey without informing me or any of you. So my calling you here is to ask for your knowledge of his whereabouts.

NIJI: Great men of Abaii, I greet you all *(clears throat)* I am happy with this gathering. On the issue at hand I will say that the elders of Obene are behind Agagu's disappearance. Yes! I have to hit the nail straight on the head, because our fathers said that "A straight path to ones destination is better even though the crooked path might touch many other areas before the final destination." Agagu's disappearance must be connected to Oghale's death. You may wonder how! But remember, Efosa and other Obene elders protested against

Oghale's execution. So Agagu disappeared due to Efosa's evil plans, this I believe. Reasons, they say are preferred to sentiments but sentiment, when properly considered could decide situations correctly.

ELOHO: Yes! It is time when sentiments stood in place of reasons. Efosa and his gang as I know them would not accept anything in exchange for Agagu since Oghale-their spokes man was hanged. Let's wait and see if they will still hold back Agagu or threaten to kill him...

NWAYE: (*interrupts*) Abomination! Can never happen!

ELOHO: Yes, you said it can never happen, but I tell you, Obene elders especially Efosa are wicked enough to take such decision.

NIJI: Then we won't accept it for any reason Agagu killed because of Oghale's death! He was condemned by the gods and hanged in the presence of everybody. Agagu can't be killed, they know we will avenge.

ITONHOSA: I only kept quiet to watch and hear what you all have to say. Let me tell you bluntly that I have investigated this issue to its very root and have got all their plans on my palm...
(*silent reaction from the elders*).

…Yes! I know what I'm saying. They've started recruiting warriors to complement those ones already down. If you doubt me, check out why Obenefe had left for Obene. That was one of Efosa's ideas! They said instead of releasing Agagu, they are ready to fight till their last man is killed. It is now left to us.

ELOHO: Wonderful! Can you see? I won't come out with any decision first. Let me hear yours before saying anything. Hmm… I hope you remember that Abaii is the son of Ababi and has the right to take strict decisions on Obene when necessary.

AUBETHE: It keeps baffling me, because I wonder what Efosa and his gang think they are up to. Do they have more warriors or is it the experience? Tell me! What do they think they're up to? Since they have prepared for war, they will have it to their satisfaction. I think they should be given what ever they want.
(silent reaction from the elders).

NIJI: *(laughs)* I said it! They were behind Agagu's disappearance. Now they're ready for war, war! What else? Aubethe has said it all. I fully support him, we should give them what they asked for, nothing less! Agiri and Efosa, think of themselves to be wise and brave, so we need to prove them

wrong and get Ababi out of this mess. Give them what they
want even if it requires Efosa's head!

ELOHO: Emm, if you support Niji's proposal, indicate by raising up
your hand…
(all the elders raise up the hands).
So we all are now in one accord. Then let us get prepared to
pounce on them furiously after fourteen days of grace.
Nwaye and Onorinode should take up training of the warriors
for the confrontation, while Itonhosa and NIji, should fashion
out plans for a successful battle. Aubethe will be the one to
go negotiate for Agagu's release. Please Aubethe, fourteen
days to free Agagu or war! *(Stops talking and leave the
palace in a fury)*
*(The elders stand to take their leave after the Oba leaves.
Music plays audibly)*.

ACT FOUR
SCENE 1

(After the fourteenth day, the following night at the Obene plains, the atmosphere is boiling anxiety is everywhere as battle music plays audibly.   On opposite sides of the plain are Abaii and Obene warriors; Abaii to the north and Obene to the south. Some men on both sides hold native burning torches with one hand and spears on the other hand. These men are half naked with some grasses around their waists, bushes on their heads and their faces painted with some river chalk.

The front liners of Abaii warriors hold on their right-hand, spears and on their left triangular shields. They are almost half naked with grasses resting on their shoulders and around their necks. Their faces have black paint and some grasses around their heels.

Behind the front warriors are others armed almost like the front liners expect for the sword as their right hand instead of spears. Also behind these, are other men with native burning torches and spears.

On the side of the Obene warriors; the frontlines are half naked with grasses on their heads and leaves and grasses around their waist. Their faces, bared chest and limbs have white paint. They hold circular shields with their left hand and spears with the right. And Behind them are other warriors with native burning torches and spears.

The battle music plays audibly. A flute sounds and the warriors face-out each other to finish. The battle continues brutally all through the night into the following day with much causality on the side of the Obene's. The flute sounds and the battle stops).

(*Music continues*).

SCENE 2

(Later that same day, at the Oba's palace, Eloho calls the elders of Abaii).

ELOHO: Great men of Abaii you are all welcome. Emm, I got some hints on what happened at the battlefield but would like Nwaye to tell us our achievements, so that we could access and know what steps to take next.

NWAYE: (*stands and clears his throat*). Great men of Abaii, your highness, I greet your all. As Aubethe said last time we were here, that he wondered what Efosa and his gang were up to. If not for a second chance Onorinode said we should give them, all Obene warriors would have been finished, because we pounded on them as the mortar pestle pounds on the yam. We thought we should give them a second chance to rethink and release Agagu or we'll pound on them. It was obvious to them that they have lost the battle. They were helpless. (*Sits majestically, feeling happy and satisfied*).

ELOHO: Wonderful! Isn't that great? What else do they need to do, rather than releasing Agagu and forward an apology which would never be accepted except Efosa and Agiri are removed from the group of Obene elders. I hereby suggest that another fourteen days of grace be offered to them to reconcile and release Agagu. Aubethe would do this.

NIJI: Great men of Abaii (*rises*). Your highness, I have heard all you have said including your suggestion. It is time that Obene should be given sometime of grace to release Agagu. It is also a good idea that after the Agagu's release, Efosa and Agiri will be asked to quit the elder's seats of Obene and Ababi. But I for one know Efosa and Agiri much more than they know themselves. It was because we over powered them that the story is still like this and we could come here as we have done. But I tell you, if that Obene warrior had over shadowed us ...ha! Things wouldn't have been as it is now. If I were you, Nwaye and Onorinode, I would have gone into Obene and got rid of Agiri and Efosa, dead or alive!
(There is sullen s*ilent from the elders and the Oba shows sign of disagreement*).
...Yes! I know what I'm saying; get Efosa and Agiri dead or alive! I know those men and what they can do! If they have found their way into Abaii! Hmm, what else, they would have murdered as many of us as possible and eventually secede as stand as a different clan. Yes of course! I know what I'm saying and I tell you, no matter the level of negotiations with Efosa and his gang, they would only remain adamant and continue to look for ways, ways to

invade us and secede! Except we remain victorious (*Sits with a troubled look on his face*).

ELOHO: Niji, I heard you and believed Nwaye and Onorinode also heard you. You are very sentimental; your feeling would be looked into. When they fail to release Agagu, then we will know that they are hunting for the impossible. They can't be victorious. If they fail to release Agagu, Nwaye and Onorinode should advance and get rid of Efosa and Agiri and also free Agagu.

ONORINODO: (*clears his throat and stands*) Emm, I heard what Niji and your highness have said. But I shouldn't be blamed since the second chance we are giving them would avail us the opportunity to plan how to capture Efosa and Agiri. Also I don't believe Obene wants to secede, so Niji may be wrong…

(*silent reactions from the elders*)

…of course yes! He may be wrong. And I assure you; we are going to remain victorious (*Sits*).

NIJI: Your highness, it seems we have saboteurs here among us. Yes! I know what I am saying. I perceive some odour of sabotage in the first battle. Onorinode and Nwaye must have connived with Efosa's men to bring Abaii down. I knew what plans Itonhosa and I did. You see, this is ridiculous!

We were ready looking for our enemies out their in the battle field with no knowledge we have some here. You see, I don't understand your plans anymore O, hmm!

NWAYE: Niji! Niji!

NIJI: No, no! Don't call me!

NWAYE: That is a child's talk; you just spoke like a child playing with a toy. You've just disappointed the world. It is a pity.

ELOHO: We must not allow confusion to crop in at this crucial time. I won't live to see Efosa victorious. I will rather die than live to see Efosa win! Everybody should return to the role assigned to him and work harder for greater success. Onorinode and Nwaye don't retreat but forge ahead to get rid of Efosa and Agiri or you'll be regarded as true saboteurs. (Stops talking and leaves. The elders leave palace in disagreement).

(*Music plays*).

SCENE 3

(Thirteen days after the first battle, at the Chief of the elder's palace, the Obene elders are gathering. Each of them dressing in the usual way but with a small black cloth tied around the neck indicating a sign of mourning).

EFOSA: Great men of Obene, I great you all. I know that we are mourning for those who lost their lives on the battlefield. Emm, we know that Abaii has been appealing for reconciliation including the release of Agagu and we've turned deaf ears to it because we want and need to. Indeed we lost some good warriors but theirs didn't go unharmed. We should not in any way settle for any compromise. Since Oghale's death was meant to revolutionize Ababi and any step to compromise would not only jeopardize it but would put an end to it. Then the gods will remain angry with us and things will go from bad to worst. Remember how things were before the war; when we had not out rightly revolted. The heads of us that were not inclined to Eloho's evil deeds were being chopped off one after the other using the gods as an excuse. How about now, when they would be going about with chips on their shoulder believing they've conquered us. How then could we escape the cold hands of death? Let's not allow the thoughts of some conditional-liberty to rob us of total freedom and better relationship with the gods of our land.

AGIRI: Great elders of Obene: Let us take heart and bear the loss of our warriors. I am happy because most of us here see things from the same perspective as I do. I am happy because we have men who can turn their vision into reality, men who have insight and whose views into the future are rather not myopic. Surrendering to Eloho is letting the death of Oghale go for nothing and turning a scapegoat for Eloho to kill whenever he wishes. Remember Obenefe, she would blame herself for accepting our plans because nothing would make her escape death! Finally, settling for a compromise would leave this land under the wrath of the gods. Then our faces would be covered with shame and our mouth padlocked not to speak when we should, only because we settled for a compromise.

OMOGEVA: Great men of Obene, we are mourning our warriors yes, but we say the best way to honour the dead is to finish that which they died for. If we are sincerely mourning our lost heroes; then let us go ahead and make possible what they fought for! This is seeing Oviemuno enthroned as the Oba of Ababi. So we need not relent but forged ahead and get Eloho out of the royal seat, strike him down. Then, Niji and his inmates will be free from the prison of their conscience.

EFOSA: Great men of Obene indeed we are great. We've spoken and heard what we said. So let us take up our assignment with enthusiasm and the gods will surely come to our aid. Tell the warriors to be determined and be confident in the battlefield. Once we over power them then, let the warriors rush to the Oba's palace and kill Eloho because that is the only way our plans would work. Remember to tell the warriors not to be afraid or discouraged for the gods are behind us.

(Music plays to indicate a mournful atmosphere as the elders take their leave).

SCENE 4

(The following night after the expiration of the dead line, at the plains of Obene. The atmosphere is very tense and full of anxiety as music of battle plays audibly.

To the north of the plain are the Abaii warriors arranged and costumed like in the first battle.

On the side of the Obene, are warriors arranged and costumed like in the first battle.

The music keeps playing. A flute sounds and the warriors face out one another. The battle grows tougher into midnight as the Abaii warriors seem to be overpowering the Obene worriors. Suddenly, the situation turns for change and what seems like a strong wind takes off the spears and shields from the hands of Abaii warriors. The Obene warriors catch on this as they advance killing the Abaii warriors, who turns and takes to their heels. The Obene warriors continue to kill the Abaii warriors as they head for the Oba's palace. An Abaii warrior runs into the Oba's palace through the front door, where he finds the Oba and two elders).

WARRIOR: Flee your highness! Flee for your life! The Obene warriors have overpowered us. They knocked down anything that seemed to block their way and they are coming to this palace for your highness. What seemed like a ghost took our shields and spears from us.

(The two elders dash out through the door behind).

ELOHO: So far so good. My tongue had almost ended my life; let darkness hang on my eyes and my mind would rest. Yes! I have worked so hard to attain this hour. Look my warrior; keep to my command, for I will never die shamefully in the hands of Efosa. I know they are coming for me. So point your spear towards me and hold it tight; while you turn away your face. For I will run into it…

(*The warrior looks amazed and confused as he obeys*)

…Yes, for I killed Oghale because I know he is fighting against me. If he has come to revenge, so be it.

(Noise of Obene warriors gets very close to the Oba's palace).

WARRIORS: Flee, your highness flee!

ELOHO: Hold your spear strongly! (*Runs into it and falls*).

(The warrior runs for his life as the Obene warriors enter the palace only to find the Oba dead with a spear stuck to his belly).

(Music showing mixed feeling plays audibly).

<h1 style="text-align:center">ACT FIVE
SCENE 1</h1>

(After four quiet days for the dead Oba, at the Chief of the elders' palace, Efosa calls the elders of Ababi convene. The men are sitting as usual. Also present are the Priest, Usoro, Omoefe and Obenefe).

EFOSA: (*clears his throat*) Great men of Abaii, great men of Obene, I greet and welcome you all to this memorable gathering of our time. First and foremost, I wish to apologize to our great elder, Agagu, for the role he was forced to play. Indeed, I have explained this to his very understanding and he accepted it but I would want him to stand up to show that spirit of acceptance for general witness…

(*Agagu stands and waves his hands and the elders give applause*).

…I also apologize to both the Obene and Abaii elders and the villages for the stress and misfortune just ended battle caused them. I pray that the gods of our land will repay us back in abundance. We have ended the battle because we know that quarrel between brothers shouldn't go deep into the bone marrow which was why I called us so that we can resolve our differences amicably and fudge ahead in peace and unity. Not that we were afraid nor fear secession, that made us stop the fighting but because we saw peace ahead after Eloho. For we say, "What an elder sees sitting, a child can't see even when standing". We are not here to boast of our achievements but to call for oneness on the plain that there was no victor and no vanquished. As the saying goes, "Just one finger, cannot remove a louse from the human hair," and we know fully well that a bird does not fly with only one wing…

THE ELDERS: Abomination!

EFOSA: Yes, not that Obene cannot go single and independent but being together would build for us a strong shield against any outside attacks.
(*The elders nod*)

NIJI: Great elders of Ababi, I great you all. I thank you for your high level understanding. We say that character is a god: it supports you according to your behaviour. I congratulate you elders of Obene once again for your insight and determination, despite the opposition from my elders and I propelled by the late Oba Eloho. But I won't leave these blames on Eloho's head alone, because our fathers say, "it is not good to talk bad about the dead." I said this because if not for the crack on the wall, the lizard won't be in it. Yes, I for one knew that Eloho wasn't meant to be the Oba but because of some selfish attitudes; Itonhosa, Agagu and I in particular allowed the crack which was done by these two women standing over there, Omoefe and Usoro. But it was all our faults and mine in particular for allowing such greedy and worthless attitudes to eat into us. Emm, I ask for mercy on behalf of all.

AGIRI: Emm... All of us present here have made up our mind to accept any apologies from you for good. Though the wounds will soon heal, the scares would remain as a fore-warning to the future generations. Yes! Our fathers say, "An elderly person won't be at home and watch the children play and blind themselves with brown sticks." We did not only watch them play and blind themselves but had allowed the same brown stick to blind us.

What then shall we do? We were there when it all happened and it is our duty as the elders around not to allow the hands of a monkey into the pot of soup. So let us not blame these women. Yes, they tempted us no doubt, but we accepted to fall into it. Our plans now should levy emphasis on how to correct the mistakes for peace, unit and progress.

ITONHOSA: Great men of Ababi, they say evil controls the mind like alcohol. Those days we talked in support of Eloho's evil deeds, it was not that we didn't know they were evil but because we had initiated ourselves into it. And stopping him was like stopping a habitual drunk from drinking. So may our apologies be whole-heartedly accepted. Indeed, our teeth have touched a bone and we have really felt it. But we must not allow the same thing that removed our teeth to blind our eyes.

OMOGEVA: Yes Itonhosa, my grand mother said, "He who tears the garment of honour wears the mask of disgrace." Eloho killed himself because, he does not want to wear the mask of disgrace, but we are all here to sew back the torn garment of honour. My great elders, if Eloho's doings were wrong, then the priest must be a liar. I believe he has come and tell us the truth. Let him come to tell us the truth because I wonder what he has to say.

PRIEST: (*walks to the space in between the elders*). Your greatness, it is a pity that I am seeing this day because the gods won't spear me. I know, if you kill me, it won't be bad because I deserve it and the gods will support you. I was put there by the late Oba, who forced me to say things I really didn't want to say. But I know that any other option was nothing but death by hanging which my predecessor did and was hanged. I would have preferred to die like that and obey the gods, but I said to myself, "some elders are in support of this and any failure to dance to their tune would mean a shameful death…"

(*silent reaction's from the elders*).

…Really, the gods wanted Oviemuno as the Oba but Eloho changed it all and forced me to say that the gods wanted

Oviemuno dead. This as you all know was what my predecessor said and was hanged. Secondly, I won't say I don't know anything about Oghale's death. Eloho did that to stop Oghale's serious opposition. There was once, when I was asked to say that the gods want Efosa and Agiri heads…
(*A look of surprise on each elder's face*).
…Yes! But that couldn't see the light of the day, there were so many other things which I cannot remember now but none of what I said then was from the gods. So I know I deserve death, no mercy but I am asking for one, even if I would be ostracized from this land but let me live.

EFOSA: (*clears his throat*). Emm, I'm sure we all heard him right. We know Eloho directed you at the threat of death, but I won't just say I pardon you, because I can't take such decisions alone here. I would suggest that since you have admitted your faults, a general opinion on your case should prevail. So if you want him pardoned and also to remain in this land, indicate by raising your right hand…
(*All the elders raise up their hands*)
Emm, I am happy you showed sympathy. So you are pardoned and can live freely in this land.

NWAYE: Emm really, I am one of Abaii elders, who supported Eloho, but I for one, thought he was doing the right thing! I heard all what you all have said, but one thing seems to be bothering me. I know you would ask, what else is it? Yes, one thing still bothers me. Before Eloho was crowned, the Priest said the gods wanted Eloho as the Oba and not Oviemuno. Later the same gods said they wanted Oviemuno dead! Later again, the gods said they wanted Oghale dead, which was done. Hmm! Now tell me, are the gods indecisive? Are they so blind that they couldn't differentiate between Oviemuno and Eloho? Or don't they keep to their words? No, reason with me and see the depth of the wound caused by these gods on us! Or rather I think I am wrong for asking those questions, may be I should have asked this one question, "We say the gods have spoken; please who are these gods?" I feel there is no need for any answer. But let it ring always in our minds and let our conscience gives us the answer, so that it could heal the wounds in us and prevent future recurrence.

AGAGU: Hmm! Wise words fill the mind with good food as it brings insight to the mind. He who does not have wisdom should endeavour to find her. The eyes know immediately what quantity of food would fill the stomach. Let us bring back the rightful person to the royal seat and let things go well with us again. We say, if one does not eat yam because of oil, one will eat oil because of yam. Let Oviemuno be the Oba.

NIJI: Great men of Ababi, let us leave it till the next market day
        and Oviemuno will be crowned the Oba and our land will see
        its glory again. Let us allow the sun to set here great men.
        (*The elders and all present leave the palace as music plays*
        audibly).

SCENE 2

(The market day is here, at the Oba's palace, the elders of Ababi are sitting as usual. The palace is full of people both young and old. Many people are also standing outside the palace. Oviemuno is standing beside the royal seat. There is a space extending from the door behind the royal seat into the palace, where the dancers are to dance around. The dancers appear briefly, apparent that they comprise some female dancers to compliment the male. Few minutes afterwards, the dancers should dance off into the door as they slacken their pace. Drumming and shouting continues quite audibly and fade away as Efosa stands).

EFOSA: Great people and elders of Ababi; young and old alike, I welcome you to this ceremony of ours…

(The villagers respond with tumultuous applause). …It may look wonderful for us to see crown changing heads within a short period of time. We know very well that after one Oba, another succeeds him. But you would ask, "Why is it Oviemuno and not Eloho's son?" And I would answer you with this similar question. Why did Eloho instead of Oviemuno succeed his father Irobosa? We know that the head destined to wear the King's crown will surely be crowned one day. Oviemuno is destined to wear the Oba's crown and will be crowned today. This is why we are here today. *(The crown cheers).*

Here he is standing beside his late father's royal seat and before us ready to serve the gods and people of Ababi. As usual, it is often preferred to hear from the horse's mouth. So I am going to ask him on your behalf the following question and he will answer them to your hearing…

(*Oviemuno steps out and stands between the two rows of the elders facing the crowd and bowing his head*)

Emm, Oviemuno, are you ready to carry the task of serving Ababi as the Oba?

OVIEMUNO: Yes, I am!

EFOSA: Can we trust in you Oviemuno, to defend and bring back the lost glory of Ababi?

OVIEMUNO: Yes, you can!

EFOSA: How about the gods of our land, will you renew the relationship between our gods and us?

OVIEMUNO: Yes, I will!

EFOSA: My dear people of Ababi, I believe you heard him right…

THE VILLAGERS: (*shouts*) Yes! Yes! We have heard him. We want him.

(Oviemuno kneels down as Efosa goes nearer to him holding the crown)

EFOSA: We can see Oviemuno, waiting to be crowned the Oba of Ababi. May he be the one who the gods want. May the gods of our land be with him, may they stand behind him in support and never oppose him. May he trample on his enemies, as his foes find their place under his feet. May his reign be gracious and splendid, let the splendour of his days from today be felt like the overhead sun, and may the gods of our fathers lead and guard him. *(Put the crown on Oviemuno's head)*.

THE VILLAGERS: Ise! Ise!!

EFOSA: Oviemuno! From today henceforth, you are our Oba, the Oba of this great land, take heed! For the fall of dead leaves from tree is nothing but a fore warning to the green ones. May your son succeed you as the next Oba of Ababi.

OVIEMUNO: Ise!

EFOSA: Fellow Ababians, it is said that he whose head was used to break a coconut does not live to eat out of it. This glorious moment could not have seen the day's light but for some heads, which are not here to witness it alive. I know that they're rejoicing in the world of the dead. So remember you those that lost their lives for today including the great Oghale.

Also, do not forget my fellow elders and me in particular for the sacrifice we took for your betterment because my days are numbered.

Be determined and confident in all you do and note that the gods will not do for you what you can do for yourself. May the gods of our land guide and see us through this difficult time to a time of plenty.

(The villages and elders bow their heads as they answer "Ise". Oviemuno goes to the royal seat, bows and sits down)

(The dancers reappear and music plays audibly as the villagers kick and stamp the floor with their feet. Everybody is obviously in a joyous mood).